GORDON
GOULD

Laser Man

Scott McPartland

D1244480

ROURKE ENTERPRISES,INC.
VERO BEACH, FLORIDA 32964

A Blackbirch Graphics book.

Library of Congress Cataloging-in-Publication Data

McPartland, Scott.
  Gordon Gould / by Scott McPartland.
    p.   cm. — (Masters of invention)
  Includes index.
  Summary: Traces the work of the physicist who finally won recognition as the inventor of lasers after a long battle to be given credit for his ideas.
    ISBN 0-86592-079-6
    1. Gould, Gordon, 1920–   —Juvenile literature. 2. Lasers—History—Juvenile literature.   3. Physicists—United States—Biography—Juvenile literature. [1. Gould, Gordon, 1920–
2. Physicists. 3. Inventors. 4. Lasers—History.] I. Title. II. Series.
QC16.G63M38   1993
621.36'6'092—dc20
[B]   93-2819
                                                                           CIP
                                                                            AC

CONTENTS

THE FORGOTTEN INVENTOR

Gordon Gould's long struggle . . . shows how refusing to give up is sometimes the only way to win.

*T*his is the story of a man named Gordon Gould, the inventor of the laser. Almost everyone has seen laser light. Most of us think the laser is the light, but it isn't. A laser is the device that makes the light and amplifies, or strengthens, it.

The word *laser* actually stands for light amplification by the stimulated omission of radiation. This is a word Gordon Gould thought up in 1957, when he invented his device. From the very beginning, Gordon knew the laser had the power to change the world. Today, there are lasers the size of your school's gymnasium that put out trillions of watts of power. There are also lasers that are so small you could line up 280,000 of them on a 12-inch ruler.

Opposite: Lasers have changed the world, but Gordon Gould had to fight a long, hard struggle to prove that he was the mastermind behind their development.

CD players use lasers to create sound. In supermarkets, lasers scan prices at the check-out. They carry perfect telephone signals across the country and make amazing light shows at rock concerts. Some lasers are so powerful that they can melt holes in sheets of steel and make things hot enough to cut, weld, or solder. Others are gentle enough to allow doctors to operate on damaged eyes safely and to vaporize harmful cancer cells without touching anything else. There is still no practical way, however, to make laser weapons. Most lasers around us wouldn't harm an ant.

Every year, industries come up with new uses for lasers. You could say that lasers are the most important invention in the last 40 years. But even if lasers didn't have so many uses, they would still be very valuable tools for science. This is because lasers make a new kind of light. Before lasers, no one ever made what is called pure light.

The inventor of such an important thing should be one of the most famous scientists alive. But few people outside his field know of Gordon Gould. Until fairly recently, hardly anyone believed he invented the laser.

If you look in an American encyclopedia or in old books about lasers, they will say that the laser was invented by Charles H. Townes and Arthur L. Schawlow. Most of the Russian encyclopedias claim that the first laser was

Lasers amplify light by exciting the atoms of certain substances. This laser was created to excite atoms within its beam in order to study how non-charged atoms collide with charged atoms (electrons).

invented by Nikilai G. Basov and Aleksandr M. Prokhorov. In 1964, Townes, Basov, and Prokhorov shared the Nobel Prize in physics for inventing the laser. The Nobel Prize is the greatest award one can receive in a given field. A committee of scientists from all over the world chooses the winners.

How could so many people be wrong about something? This book will explain how Gordon Gould invented the laser in 1957 and why it took almost 30 years for him to be recognized as the laser's creator. The reasons have a lot to do with how modern science works. Part of this involves getting a patent, an official document giving an inventor the sole right to make, use, or sell his invention. It also involves establishing priority. Priority means getting the proper credit as the discoverer or inventor of something.

Gordon Gould's long struggle for priority took courage and amazing determination. It shows how refusing to give up is sometimes the only way to win.

CHAPTER TWO

THE EARLY YEARS

"Somehow it [being an inventor] was in my blood."

*G*ordon Gould was born in New York City, on July 17, 1920. His parents were Kenneth and Helen Gould. Young Gordon got his interest in mechanical things from his mother. She gave him an erector set when he was very little. His mother used to make things with the erector set to see if Gordon could figure out how to take them apart. In a few years, he was putting things together for *her* to take apart.

Growing up, Gordon and his brothers were all interested in mechanical things. Gordon took radios apart and fixed clocks. By the time he was in high school, he knew that he wanted to be an inventor. "Somehow, it was in my blood," he said.

From an early age, Gordon was encouraged by his mother to build and create. His mother used to build structures from pieces in an erector set and then see if her young son could figure out how to take them apart.

But when Gordon was growing up, America was in the midst of the Great Depression. Times were hard. People were poor and homeless. Even people with jobs suffered.

A Desire to Succeed

Like many people who grew up during the Depression, Gordon had a strong desire for success. He dreamed of being rich and decided that inventing would make him rich.

To make his longtime dream of inventing real, Gordon studied physics at Union College in Schenectady, New York. There he was inspired by one of his professors, Dr. Frank Studer. Gordon says that he fell "in love with light at Union College."

He graduated in 1941 with a degree in physics. Right away he got a job in the test lab at Western Electric in New Jersey. This company did a variety of communication and electricity research.

The people at Western Electric liked Gordon a lot. Soon, supervisors came to introduce themselves. Every week Gordon met someone in a higher position. Finally he met the vice-president in charge of his plant.

Gordon noticed that every supervisor was older and grayer than the one before. He figured that at a big company like Western Electric he would have to wait until someone died so he could get promoted.

This didn't seem like a good way to spend his life. Gordon also didn't enjoy following other people's rules. He wanted to work in a place where he decided what projects to do. He wanted to work in a lively place full of new ideas.

Gordon also learned that people who work for big companies never get rich. He decided the only way to get rich and do the kind of work he wanted to do was to own his own company. To do this, he needed more education. After one summer at Western Electric, Gordon finally decided to never work for a big company again.

Gordon then enrolled in Yale University to get an advanced degree in physics, known as a doctorate, or Ph.D. He spent only two years at Yale, but it was a valuable time for him. He said that the experience contributed to his ability, many years later, to think of the laser. This was also where Gordon met his wife.

Gordon always had natural mechanical ability. As a teenager, he was constantly tinkering with design ideas and taking things apart to see how they worked.

Work on the Atomic Bomb

As a result of America's entry into World War II in late 1941, Gordon's career took on a new direction.

America was fighting Nazi Germany, whose scientists were among the best in the world. America was afraid that German scientists would invent terrible new weapons. Their fears were well grounded. It was soon learned that Germany was working on a secret weapon, an atomic bomb. It was important to beat Germany to this bomb. If the Germans succeeded in making their bomb, they would kill millions of people and win the war.

The United States got the best scientists from all over the free world to build an atomic bomb. They called it the Manhattan Project. One of the scientists they asked to help was Gordon Gould.

This was a very great honor. Gordon was only 23 years old. He would be working with the greatest experts on matter and energy. But it meant that his education was finished. Yale gave Gordon a master's degree, but he lost the chance to get his Ph.D.

Two years later, the Manhattan Project made a bomb that had incredible destructive ability. Many historians believe that the atomic bomb made the war end faster and saved a million lives on both sides.

Gordon was asked by the U.S. government to join the Manhattan Project in 1941, after America entered World War II. As a member of the research and development team, Gordon worked with some of the world's most brilliant scientists to create an atomic bomb.

In just three years, scientists and engineers had done something that many people had previously believed was impossible. The Manhattan Project showed what could be done when the government organized scientists and gave them as much money as they needed to succeed. This became the model for modern science. The Manhattan atomic-bomb project permanently changed how science worked.

Gordon Meets His Rival

After the war, Gordon and his wife moved to New York, where he worked for an optical-research company, Semon Bache. Two years later, he also started teaching physics at the City College of New York, one of the best public colleges in America. In 1950, he gave up working at Semon Bache and spent all his workday at City College.

Gordon was an instructor, the lowest level of college teacher. Without a Ph.D. it would be hard to advance in a college career. Finally, in 1954, Gordon left City College to become a research assistant at New York's Columbia University and finish his Ph.D. There were six future Nobel Prize winners at Columbia. One of them was Charles H. Townes, the man who would one day unjustly get the credit for Gordon's invention of the laser.

Townes was only five years older than Gordon, but he was a leader in physics. At 24, Townes got his Ph.D. from the California Institute of Technology. His first research job was at Bell Telephone Laboratories, where he did various projects on radar for the U.S. Air Force.

In 1943, Townes became a professor at Columbia and the director of the university's radiation laboratory. As a result of his unique experimentation there, Townes developed the maser. The word *maser* stands for microwave amplification by stimulated emission of radiation. The idea behind the maser is similar to that of the laser, so the work that went into developing the maser was also important to building the first laser.

With the maser's extremely accurate vibrations, Townes developed the atomic clock, the best instrument for keeping time ever invented. It was accurate to one second every 300 years.

Townes soon became head of the physics department at Columbia. He was a perfect model of success, a powerful force in the world of physics, and a natural-born leader.

CHAPTER THREE

A BREAKTHROUGH

"He knew right away that the laser would be the most important thing he would ever be involved with."

*A*lthough Charles Townes and Gordon Gould were destined to be rivals, Gordon didn't work under Townes while he was at Columbia. His supervisor was Polykarp Kusch. Kusch was not interested in practical ideas. All he was interested in was doing research.

Kusch studied how matter gave off energy, especially how stimulated (excited) matter emitted radiation. For three years, Gordon experimented with an atomic-beam machine. His task was to excite an element called thallium, a metal used in the production of infrared detectors and optical glass.

None of Gordon's ways to keep thallium atoms stimulated worked. One day, another professor, I.I. Rabi, suggested a new technique called optical pumping. This was the breakthrough Gordon needed. He later said that it was this important work, plus his previous research and development at Yale, that prepared him for developing the laser.

While he was working out his ideas for the development of a laser, Gordon worked with an atomic-beam machine that excited the atoms in an element called thallium. It was that work that eventually pointed him in the right direction for inventing lasers.

Gordon was not the only one at Columbia working on the stimulated emission of radiation. Townes, Rabi, and Gordon Gould all had a lasing medium (something to excite atoms) and an excitation source (something to pump energy into the lasing medium), two of the three requirements for making a laser.

Gordon wondered about new ways to use stimulated emission of radiation. He was sure the next step would be amplifying light. Over the next few years, he worked with thallium atoms and thought about how to harness the excited photons (little bundles of energy, of which light is composed).

One Saturday night, November 11, 1957, Gordon suddenly thought of adding something called an optical resonator to a tube that has mirrored ends. The resonator, called a Fabry-Perot, was the way to make amplified light. This was the missing, or third, element needed to make a laser!

Gordon felt "electrified" by his discovery. After 20 years of hard work, it had all suddenly come together in one inspired moment.

Although it was late, Gordon couldn't sleep. He started writing down his ideas and drawing sketches. Right away he thought of the name *laser*. He wrote it on the top of the page describing his device.

Gordon realized that a laser could heat an object to temperatures hotter than the sun in just a few seconds. This meant lasers could create atomic energy—not in the way that an atomic bomb releases energy by splitting atoms, but the way that the sun creates energy by superheating matter.

All that night Gordon kept working. He was scribbling notes and drawing pictures in his notebook as fast as he could. He had to get his ideas on paper while his inspiration lasted. Inspiration poured out of him. He worked the whole weekend on his invention and its significance.

Those two days changed Gordon's entire life. He knew right away that the laser would be the most important thing he would ever be involved with. Eventually, his notebook would be one of the most valuable books every written. Today it is worth about one hundred million dollars. It took the world 30 years to realize its value and to make Gordon's vision come true.

A few days later, Gordon took his notebook to a nearby candy store. The owner was a notary public, someone who is allowed to witness legal documents. Gordon had him officially see the contents of the notes and drawings and put his notary stamp on the notebook. He thought that making his plans legal documents would protect them.

When Gordon had finally figured out the puzzle to making his laser work, he wrote down his designs and plans in a notebook. In an effort to safeguard his invention, he had the notebook stamped by an official witness, called a notary public.

Gordon Leaves Columbia

Soon after that weekend, Charles Townes called Gordon. Townes and a visiting professor, Arthur Schawlow (who eventually married Townes's sister, Aurelia), were also thinking about ways to create amplified light. Townes asked Gordon to explain some of his research with thallium.

As they talked, Gordon realized that Townes and Schawlow were working on ideas like his. But he didn't think they had a full plan. He figured they were months behind him. Still, he decided to act fast on his idea.

Although Gordon had always dreamed of being an inventor, until that day in 1957, he had never invented anything. All of his past experiences studying, working, teaching and experimenting prepared him for imagining the laser, but not what to do next. His steps were unknown.

Professor Kusch, Gordon's research supervisor at Columbia had no use for inventions unless they helped research. He didn't care about selling anything. As long as Gordon worked under Kusch he would never be able to develop his idea.

Gordon wanted to finish his Ph.D. He also wanted to develop the laser and become a millionaire. He couldn't do both. Finally, in early 1958, he dropped out of school and joined the Technical Research Group, or TRG for short.

TRG was small. It didn't have the rules and levels of supervisors that Western Electric and Semon Bache had. Gordon believed that TRG would let him be his own boss.

Gordon's plan was to build the laser and then return to Columbia to complete his Ph.D. He did not imagine anything could go wrong.

CHAPTER FOUR

STOLEN DREAMS

"Other scientists were making his dreams come true."

*S*omehow Gordon Gould got the idea that he needed to build a laser before he could get a patent. This was incorrect. He also thought that by having a notary stamp his notebook he had proof that he was the inventor, or had priority. This was true, but it would take a long, long time to prove that to others.

Normally, science priority is established in one of two ways. The first is by publishing an article in a respected scientific journal. A scientific journal is a magazine that is written just for scientists. Being the first person to publish on a subject establishes your claim to that idea or discovery.

Sometimes two people have the same idea at the same time. For example, Isaac Newton and Gottfried Leibniz invented the mathematical field of calculus at about the same time. However, Newton beat Leibniz on calculus because he published first. Today, we know that both men deserve credit, but it took a few centuries of argument to settle this.

The other way to get priority is with a patent. Before there was a patent office, people were always stealing each other's ideas and inventions. The only way an inventor could protect something was by keeping it a secret, but secrets slow scientific progress.

So in 1790, the United States established a patent office to document who invented what. It must make sure no earlier idea is the same as a new patent. In addition, it must decide if the idea is practical. If someone sends in an application for a car that runs on water, the Patent Office doesn't issue a patent until it makes sure the idea works. It helps if the inventor submits a working model. But if the idea is too expensive to build, detailed plans are enough.

Patent applications are carefully dated. Sometimes two people submit similar ideas. Then the process becomes like a race. The first person to get a patent wins. This is what happened with Nikola Tesla and Guglielmo Marconi, who separately invented the radio.

Unaware of the proper procedures for getting a legal patent, Gordon was unable to secure his rightful ownership of the laser when it was first perfected.

Marconi beat Tesla because Marconi filed first for the patent. But both men had valid claims. When people feel the Patent Office has made a mistake, they must sue the other person in court. Tesla sued Marconi, but by the time the case was decided, Tesla was dead—winning did him no good.

Once the Patent Office rules, a license is given to the inventor. For the next 17 years, anyone who uses the invention must pay the inventor. This is called a royalty. After that, anyone can use or change the invention.

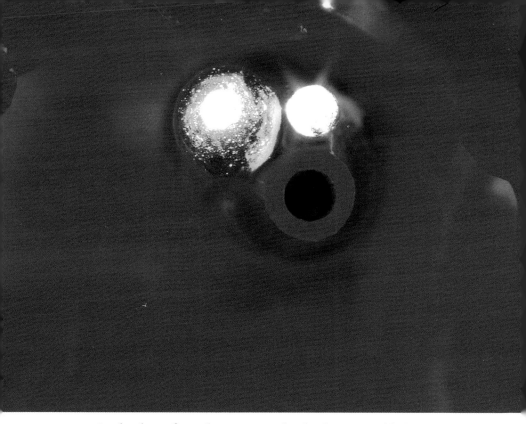

Gordon knew from the very start that his lasers would change the world in a dramatic way. Lasers used for medical purposes—such as this one breaking down hard deposits inside the arteries of a human heart—have enabled doctors to perform thousands of new procedures.

A Big Mistake

In one way it was too bad Gordon was not working under Charles Townes. Townes was on the editorial board of two journals, *Physical Review* and the *Journal of Chemical Physics.* Townes also had a patent on the maser and could have helped Gordon publish or shown him how to apply for a patent.

But because Gordon mistakenly believed that he had to make a laser before he could patent his idea, he wanted to keep his idea a secret. While he was working on his laser at TRG, the company tried to get government contracts to pay for his work.

At first no one wanted to give TRG money. Gordon spent another year developing his notebooks. He wrote plans for a gas-discharge laser and several other things. One was a special switch, called a Q switch. It would release the energy of a laser in one "giant pulse" of light. The other was Brewster angle windows, openings for the laser beam to travel through without losing too much energy.

Gordon also worked on ways to use the laser. He wrote in his notebooks about using lasers for drilling, weapons, and energy. He had a strong feeling about the ways lasers could improve people's lives.

Gordon Is Banned from TRG

More than a year passed. During that time, Townes and Schawlow worked on their invention, and in December of 1958, they wrote the first paper on the laser. They didn't call it a laser, though. They called their device an optical maser. They were about a year behind Gordon, but they won the race to publish, a race Gordon didn't even know he was in.

In 1959, Townes left Columbia to become the director of research at the Institute for Defense Analyses in Washington, D.C. In June

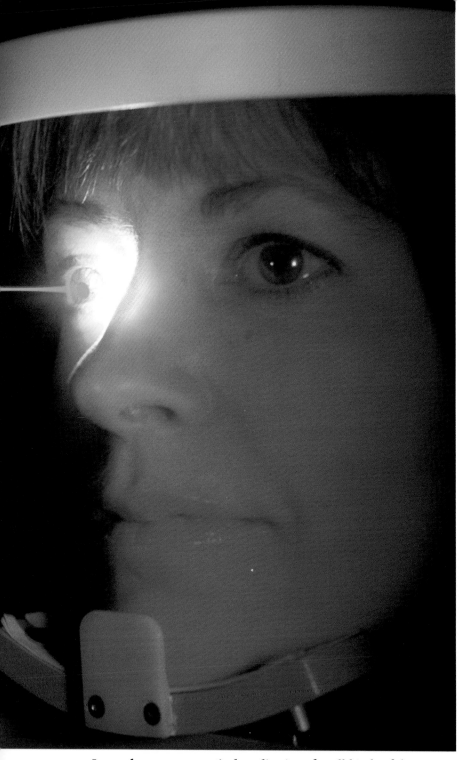

Lasers have many practical applications for all kinds of doctors. Here, a laser is used to scan and treat a patient's eye.

of 1959, Townes and Schawlow applied for a patent on the optical maser.

At about the same time, TRG finally got a contract. Gordon's idea to use the laser for drilling and creating weapons impressed the U.S. Department of Defense. TRG asked for $300,000 to develop the laser. The government liked the idea so much that it offered TRG one million dollars instead. But it put a big condition on the contract. Gordon wasn't allowed to work on any project involving the Department of Defense.

Laser technology has been developed by the U.S. government for everything from surveillance devices to weapons to anti-missile detection units. Here, an anti-missile free-electron laser is assembled in a laboratory.

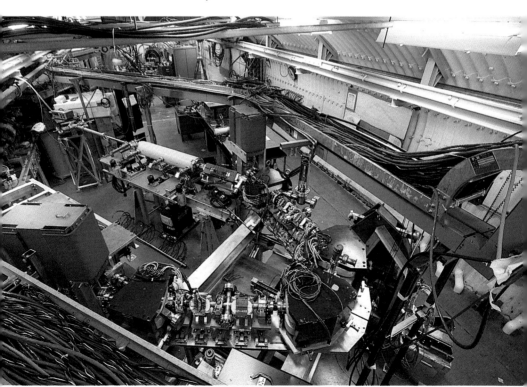

The reason is somewhat involved. During World War II, the United States and Russia fought together against Germany. Russia was a Communist country. Most Americans do not approve of the Communist way of life. But because America was more worried about beating Germany than anything else, it didn't view communism as a threat then.

After the war, however, America and Russia became bitter enemies. Certain people in the government felt that anyone who studied communism was an enemy, too. Since Gordon and his wife had attended meetings about communism while he was at Yale, the Department of Defense banned him from TRG. It also took his notebooks, labeling them "secret documents."

Other Inventors Forge Ahead

Gordon and TRG had a good idea, but they did not have a working model of a laser. There were many problems yet to solve. And before they could sell lasers, they needed to make one.

Gordon's friends at TRG were not allowed to tell him about the project. They could call him up and ask questions. But they couldn't say what the questions were about. This made it hard for TRG to make progress. Only Gordon really understood his notebooks. Without

As soon as Gordon and his colleagues made their inventions public, many other scientists and researchers began to study the possible uses and properties of lasers.

his direction, the work at TRG would take much longer.

Since Gordon was not allowed to work at TRG, he had free time to apply for a patent. He knew that this would be hard without his notebooks or a working laser and he didn't realize that Townes and Schawlow had applied nine months earlier.

One of TRG's big problems was finding a practical lasing medium. (Researchers needed a material that gave back as much of the energy they put in it as possible.) Some scientists believed that synthetic (human-made) ruby crystals would be good. Schawlow and Townes used rubies in the maser. Researchers at TRG spent months studying ways to make synthetic crystals. They even invited Schawlow to talk to them about it. Schawlow said rubies could not give back the energy needed for light. TRG gave up rubies. This set the company back even further in its race to make the first practical laser.

Other people were getting close to the breakthrough that Gordon, and then Townes, had. One of them was Theodore Maiman, a scientist at Hughes Aircraft Research. In May 1960, Maiman demonstrated the first amplified light. He called his invention a laser.

Maiman used a flash lamp to excite atoms inside a synthetic ruby crystal as his lasing medium. He knew that rubies would be good.

Aside from all their practical applications in science and defense, lasers can also provide stunning light shows and visual displays, such as this one at a Hollywood movie studio.

After more than a year of measuring and studying them, he decided rubies would be about 95 percent efficient.

Townes and Schawlow had been the first to publish an article outlining a form of the laser theory. Now Maiman was first to successfully demonstrate a laser. It was beginning to look as though Gordon would never get credit as the true father of the laser.

Big Companies Get In On the Action

Soon things started to look even worse for Gordon. People everywhere were fast moving ahead in the field of lasers. Companies like General Electric and Bell Telephone turned their attention to lasers. These giant corporations had much more money and personnel than small firms like TRG.

Three top Bell scientists spent two years studying helium-neon gas as a possible lasing medium. These gases proved to be excellent lasing mediums. Other early lasers, like Maiman's, could work for only a fraction of a second. They released their energy in a short burst and then had to build up again. But gas lasers could operate continually. This made them practical work tools.

The Bell scientists also discovered that lasers could carry sound waves. The problem, however, was that their laser was too big. A telephone with a laser in it would be as big as a television set.

Then, in 1962, scientist Robert Hall at General Electric made a semiconductor laser. It was smaller than a grain of salt, and its beam was very focused. Now using lasers to send voices or computer data became practical.

Something else was needed first. Laser signals could not be sent along wires. They had to travel on tubes made of glass, silicon, or

plastic called fiber-optic cables. A fiber-optic
cable is about half the diameter of a human
hair. Charles Kao, a scientist at International
Telephone and Telegraph invented it.

The combination of semiconductor lasers
and fiber-optic cables totally changed the face
of communication. Telephone cables were
once 4 1/2 inches in diameter and carried 900
conversations about a mile. The new semiconductor cables are 1/2 inch in diameter and
carry 500,000 conversations all over the world.

**You can probably see lasers in a number of places you go
every day. Many supermarkets and department stores have
installed laser-driven checkout systems that read bar codes
on products and send them directly to the cash register.**

In 1963, another Bell Labs inventor, C. K. N. Patel made the first carbon-dioxide laser. Like the helium-neon laser, it operated continually. But the carbon-dioxide laser made infrared light.

Carbon-dioxide lasers became the most useful kind of industrial lasers. They could weld or solder, tunnel through rock, or burn a hole in steel.

All the things Gordon Gould dreamed of were becoming possible. The only problem was that it was all the other scientists that were making his dreams come true.

CHAPTER FIVE

GORDON'S LONG FIGHT

*"To suddenly stop worrying about money at all
is a feeling I'm not used to."*

*D*uring these many advances made by other scientists, Gordon was still idle. He couldn't work at TRG—and they still had his notebooks. Townes and Schawlow had gotten credit for the laser. Bell Labs was getting all the royalties.

But like Tesla, Gordon still had one choice. He could sue. Maybe a court would rule his notebooks were proof of priority. It was his last chance. For the next 17 years, Gordon spent a lot of time in court.

The Courts Rule Against Gordon

In the 1960s Gordon lost all his cases. The courts ruled his claim was not valid. They decided each case individually, but Gordon always heard the same basic reasons.

The courts said that Gordon's notebooks lacked enough information for someone to build a laser with them. They pointed out that TRG failed to build a laser using Gordon's plans. This, they said, proved that Gordon's ideas did not work.

The courts ruled that Gordon had not tried hard enough to develop the laser. He had not been "diligent." In a way, they blamed him for TRG's failures, even though he had not been allowed to supervise their projects.

Court cases are very expensive. Gordon was fighting giant companies that had enormous resources, teams of lawyers, and dozens of expert witnesses. Not only that, but he was fighting accepted scientific opinion.

Charles Townes left Washington for the Massachusetts Institute of Technology, one of the finest science and engineering schools in the world. He was fast becoming even more respected. In 1964, he won the Nobel Prize in physics for his work on the maser and the laser. This showed that the world scientific community believed Townes and Schawlow. They had accomplished so much that it was reasonable to support them. But it was unfair.

Gordon was now in his forties. His court battles drove him deeply into debt. So far, his idea for the laser had brought him nothing but unhappiness, disappointment, and a great sense of frustration.

Because lasers have so many possible uses, the future of laser technology is wide open. Already, communications companies have greatly improved their capabilities with laser-based fiber-optic cables. And audio-visual technologies—such as CD players, VCRs, and televisions— have advanced rapidly by using lasers in their designs.

Many people believed Gordon was suing just to make money. Townes and Schawlow thought the matter was settled when they wrote their article. Publishing risked their reputations. If the idea had been wrong, people would have called them fools. So they deserved the credit when the laser worked.

One can believe that Gordon really had invented the laser because he did not give up. Someone who sues just to make money would not continue fighting after years of losing.

Only someone who really believed in his cause would bear so much hardship and rejection. Gordon says that he never lost confidence that someday he would win his fight. He looked at his court battles as "an interesting adventure."

In 1967, a company called Control Data bought TRG. Gordon was paid $300,000 for his share of TRG, which helped with his debt. Gordon also bought a cruising boat. Every year he sailed to the Caribbean. This made him happy because there it seemed he could forget his troubles for a while.

Support for Gordon

When TRG merged with Control Data, Gordon was free to do other things. He decided to teach again, this time at the Polytechnic Institute of New York in Brooklyn, New York. Some of his research team from TRG joined him. Gordon and his friends worked at Polytechnic until 1974.

After 10 years of setbacks, things started getting better. In 1971, Gordon became the president of the Laser Institute of America. In 1972, a lower court decided that Gordon really had invented the optically pumped laser that Irwin Wieder of Westinghouse Electric had patented in 1968.

This was a step forward and Gordon was closer to proving his claim. The 1972 decision didn't say he invented the laser, but it did affirm he was an important part of the laser's early development.

Also, in 1974, Gordon started a new company called Optelecom. This company made laser illuminators and optical cables. Gordon was finally his own boss at a promising and successful company.

This success was good, because Gordon still remained far away from collecting any laser money. In the early 1970s, every time he won a case, the companies that made lasers appealed. An appeal asks a higher court to overturn the lower-court ruling. In the meantime, the lower-court decision is set aside, which means that nothing happens.

Appeals take years. Lawyers review the case to find some mistake in the lower-court's ruling. Then a higher court tries the case all over again.

The companies that sell lasers make hundreds of millions of dollars a year. Townes's patent would expire in 1976. After that, companies could market any laser ideas without paying for them. If Gordon won his case, they would have to start paying all over again for another 17 years and Gordon would collect royalties on 80 percent of all the lasers sold in the United States and Canada.

In 1974, Gordon got a major ally when Eugene Lang became interested in helping him. Lang was very rich. He had a company called Refac Technology Development Corporation. Lang offered to pay Gordon's court costs if they split the royalties on the laser. Gordon agreed.

Lang has strong feelings about using his money to do good things. Once, while giving a speech at his old public school, he promised any student in the auditorium who graduated from high school a free college education. Today, dozens of those students are going to college for free.

Victory at Last

With Lang's help, Gordon had enough money to fight in court properly. In 1977, the appeal on the Wieder case was finally decided. Again Gordon won. Now the Patent Office had to give Gordon a laser patent.

After years of being the forgotten inventor of the laser, Gordon was getting credit for his work. In 1978, the Patent Office Society named him Inventor of the Year. Twenty-one years after his discovery, and 18 years after the first laser demonstration, Gordon Gould was finally accepted as the inventor of the laser.

Gordon's old school, Union College, honored him with the Ph.D. that he had wanted for so long. Union was proud of his victory and proud of playing a part in his education.

In 1983, Gordon won the Philadelphia City Trust award. Articles were also being written about him. Books about lasers were being revised to include him.

But not all the attention was welcome. Many people called him up with crazy invention ideas or asked him for money. Other people called every time they read something about lasers that worried them.

There were still court battles going on. This time the Patent Office was on Gordon's

With the help of an investor who paid legal fees, Gordon was finally able to win his legal cases in 1977. Within months of his victory, he established himself as the rightful owner of the laser patent.

Although the road to success was filled with frustration and disappointment, Gordon Gould never gave up. The reward for his determination was a place in history as one of the most important inventors of the twentieth century.

side. Gordon and Lang raised more money to start another company called Patlex. They wanted Patlex to help inventors fight for the rights to ideas that had been taken away from them. Gordon Gould was the first, but Patlex is looking for other inventors to help, too.

One by one, the court cases all supported Gordon and laser companies finally began to pay him royalties. In 1986, he won the final appeal about the optical pump and in 1987, he was granted royalties on the gas-discharge laser. In 1988, Gordon also got the patent on his Brewster angle windows.

Gordon was now enormously rich, but he found it strange. He said "to suddenly stop worrying about money at all is a feeling I'm not used to." He bought an expensive car and a new house. He was 66 years old when he finally retired from Optelecom and settled down to enjoy the rest of his life.

Despite all the honors and the wealth that Gordon has obtained, he still feels a little sad that he did not win the Nobel Prize for his work. He knows, however, that he is lucky to have lived long enough to see the fight for his invention through to the end.

GLOSSARY

fiber-optic cables Superthin tubes of glass, silicon, or plastic through which lasers can travel.

laser A device that amplifies, focuses, and strengthens light.

notary public A person who is authorized to act as an official witness and to make certain documents legal.

patent An official document from the government that gives an inventor the sole right to produce, use, and sell an invention.

photons Little bundles of energy that make up light.

priority The proper credit given to an inventor or person who discovered something important.

royalty Money paid to the inventor or creator of a given work.

thallium A metal used in the production of infrared light detectors and optical glass.

FOR FURTHER READING

Aaseng, Nathan. *Inventors: Nobel Prizes in Chemistry, Physics, and Medicine.* Minneapolis, MN: Lerner, 1988.

Billings, Charlene W. *Lasers: The Technology of Light.* New York: Facts On File, 1992.

Graham, Ian. *Lasers and Holograms.* New York: Franklin Watts, 1991.

Johnson, Jim. *Lasers.* Austin, TX: Raintree Steck-Vaughn, 1985.

Nardo, Don. *Lasers: Humanity's Magic Light.* San Diego, CA: Lucent, 1990.

INDEX

Photo Credits: